TREASURE HUNTS! TREASURE HUNTS!

LENNY HORT
ILLUSTRATED BY CARY PILLO

HarperCollinsPublishers

Library of Congress Cataloging-in-Publication Data
Hort, Lenny.
Treasure hunts! Treasure hunts! by Lenny Hort.
p. cm.
Includes bibliographical references.
Summary: Provides instructions for setting up and carrying out a variety of
treasure hunts and scavenger hunt games and includes treasure-related facts
and puzzles.
ISBN 0-688-17245-8 (trade)   ISBN 0-688-17177-X (pbk.)
1. Treasure hunt (Game)—Juvenile literature.
[1. Treasure hunts. 2. Games.] I. Title.
II. Title: Treasure hunts! Treasure hunts!
GV1202.T7 H67 2000
796.1'4 21—dc21   99-042371

10 9 8 7 6 5 4 3 2 1
First edition, 2000
❖
Visit us on the World Wide Web!
www.harperchildrens.com

TREASURE HUNTS! TREASURE HUNTS!

CONTENTS

TREASURE HUNTS! TREASURE HUNTS!

INTRODUCTION

Want to go treasure hunting? Tommy Thompson did.

He organized an expedition that discovered the wreck of the <u>Central America,</u> a ship that sank in eight thousand feet of water with hundreds of people and tons of gold from the California gold rush on board. Pioneering new techniques of underwater exploration, Thompson and his crew recovered treasures and historic artifacts valued in the hundreds of millions of dollars. It took them only six years and twelve million dollars—plus another seven years to fight off lawsuits from companies that claimed to have insured the treasure back in 1857.

If that sounds like too much trouble, try this book. You'll find dozens of treasure hunt and scavenger hunt games that you can play with friends and family. Some are simple, and some are tricky, but none will cost you years of work or millions of dollars' worth of equipment, and no one will sue you for a share of the treasure. You'll also find facts about real-life treasures, as well as a scattering of riddles and clues to lead you on a worldwide scavenger hunt to famous places.

If you're old enough to read this, you're probably old enough to organize most of the hunts yourself. Many are also fine for younger children, and sometimes you may find it more exciting to ask a grown-up to hide the treasure. Some hunts are designed for parties, while others can be thrown together anytime you and a friend are looking for something to do. There's plenty to choose from whether you live in a house or an apartment, and there's even a whole chapter full of hunts you can play from the backseat of a car.

I've kept the rules flexible so you can make each hunt your own. The players can hunt together or split into teams or hunt by themselves. Go right ahead and change the rules, as long as everyone knows what the rules are and nobody tries to change them in the middle of a game. I'll feel I've really struck gold if this book helps give you ideas for inventing games of your own.

Happy hunting!

A NOTE ON SAFETY

Take a commonsense approach to safety when planning treasure hunts, especially if younger children are involved. Think twice before hiding treasures or clues anyplace that might be dangerous, whether under a traffic cone in the middle of a highway or inside the nest of an endangered species of cobra halfway up the face of a rocky cliff. If a hunt is going to send players wandering far afield, they'll be safer in pairs or teams. If your parents have told you never to play in the abandoned chemical factory on Mortuary Street, then let all the players know that the abandoned chemical factory on Mortuary Street is out-of-bounds.

HUNTING FOR HIDDEN OBJECTS

Treasure hunters search a room or yard for a bunch of hidden objects, such as Easter eggs, toys, or peanuts—no clues required. Even preschoolers can join in these easy-to-organize hunts, since no reading is necessary, but they're fun for all ages.

Fossil Hunt

You'll really dig hunting for toy dinosaurs.

WHO CAN PLAY

Any number and any age.

WHERE TO PLAY

Indoors or out.

WHAT YOU'LL NEED

- Paper or plastic bags for every player or team.
- Plastic toy dinosaurs, mammoths, and other prehistoric creatures that are about two or three inches long. Ten to fifteen hidden toys should be fine for up to five treasure hunters. For larger groups, aim to have at least two or three treasures per kid. (Of course, the game works just as well with any other kind of plastic or wooden toy.)

Mini-dinosaurs, which can be bought for less than a dollar each, make great prizes and favors for birthday parties.

SETTING UP

Take five or ten minutes to hide all the toys in different places. Try to keep track of where you hide them. Indoors or out, set a clearly defined limit for where the fossils can or can't be hidden, and let all the players know what the boundaries are. Your parents will not appreciate it if eager treasure hunters turn a flower bed into a mudhole.

Good outdoor hiding places include flowerpots, fences, holes in stone walls, drainpipe openings, and notches on trees. Hide some toys off the ground; dangle a tyrannosaurus from a trellis or the bottom of a tabletop. Make sure, however, that no treasures are out of reach of the shortest person playing. Scatter a few randomly through the grass—sometimes these are the hardest of all to spot. Don't bury the fossils where no one can find them. Instead try to place each creature so that most of it is hidden, but a small part can be seen if you look very carefully.

Indoors you can avoid a mess by declaring the insides of drawers, cabinets, and garbage cans off-limits. Decide whether fossils can be hidden all over the house or just in one or two rooms. If anyone in your family doesn't want a bunch of people poking around her room, respect that. Good indoor hiding places might include napkin holders, chair bottoms, refrigerator magnets, picture frames, and bookcases, as well as under couches, rugs, and pillows.

SAFETY

Use common sense to make sure nothing gets hidden anyplace dangerous. No brontosauruses in the barbecue, no iguanodons in the insecticide, no elasmosauruses in the electrical outlets. Forget about the cat's litter box or the compost heap; they're hotbeds of bacteria. In fact, it's a good idea for all players to wash their hands after any outdoor treasure hunt.

TIPS FOR HUNTERS

Treasure hunters use their eyes and their brains. Watch for things that look out of place, like bumps in the rug, cups turned over, or rocks that aren't quite lying flat. Look up as well as down, don't stay in one spot, and keep scanning from side to side. Point your toes out, and drag your feet slowly through the grass; you might step onto a stegosaurus that others have stepped over.

HOW TO PLAY

Decide whether players should hunt on their own or split up into teams. If preschoolers are mixed in with older players, then teams are usually best, and the older kids should try to make sure that every younger kid finds at least one treasure of his own. Remind the players which areas are in and which are out-of-bounds, and let the hunt begin.

If all the treasures haven't been found in fifteen or twenty minutes, it's okay to start giving out hints if all the players agree and if clues are given out fairly to everyone. You can announce that fossils are still waiting to be found in certain areas, or even tell players whether they're getting warmer or colder. Or let everyone know that you can see a treasure or two from the spot where you're standing. If anything still hasn't been found after half an hour, give a two-minute warning; then end the game, and show where the missing fossils were hidden. Whichever player or team has found the most is the winner and can decide whether they want a turn at hiding the toys again for another treasure hunt.

WORLDWIDE SCAVENGER HUNT

Solve the clues, rhymes, and riddles scattered throughout the book to search the world for some famous landmarks and national treasures! Can you set a global treasure hunt for your friends?

—1—
Worldwide Scavenger Hunt
A lady in a long green gown
with seven points upon her crown
came from France to New York town.
(Answer found on p. 80)

15

Fossil Feud

In this fossil hunt, every player gets the fun of hiding treasures—and the fun of hunting for them.

WHO CAN PLAY

Any number and any age.

WHERE TO PLAY

Indoors or out.

WHAT YOU'LL NEED

- At least twelve to twenty plastic dinosaurs or other toys that are about two to three inches long.
- A paper or plastic bag for every player or team.

HOW TO PLAY

If there are more than two players, split into two teams. Give each team an equal number of fossil toys to hide. Each team goes into a different room or outdoor area where the other team can't see them and hides all the toys. Then the teams switch places and try to find the fossils that the other team has hidden. Whoever finds all the other side's fossils first—or whoever finds the most fossils in thirty minutes—is the winner.

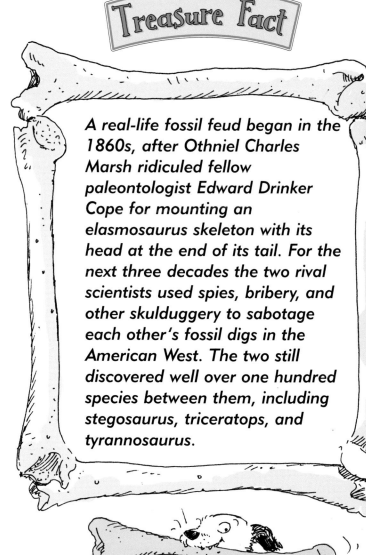

Treasure Fact

A real-life fossil feud began in the 1860s, after Othniel Charles Marsh ridiculed fellow paleontologist Edward Drinker Cope for mounting an elasmosaurus skeleton with its head at the end of its tail. For the next three decades the two rival scientists used spies, bribery, and other skulduggery to sabotage each other's fossil digs in the American West. The two still discovered well over one hundred species between them, including stegosaurus, triceratops, and tyrannosaurus.

Coin Hunt

Hunting for pennies is loads of fun, and they don't cost as much as toy dinosaurs. Finding them is a thrill for younger children, but toddlers are too young for this game; they might put the coins in their mouths and choke. A good game is to give two teams twenty-five or fifty pennies each, then let the teams hide their coins and hunt for the other team's coins, as in Fossil Feud.

Treasure Fact

Serious treasure hunters from all over the world compete at coin shooting: hunting for hidden coins and other buried treasures with metal detectors.

Peanut Hunt

The local squirrels and elephants will clean up after you when you stage this hunt that has been a favorite at parties for at least a hundred years.

WHO CAN PLAY

Any number and any age.

WHERE TO PLAY

Outdoors or in.

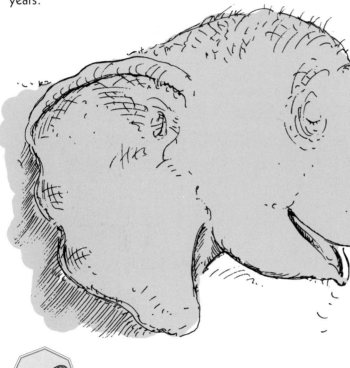

SAFETY

Some people are dangerously allergic to peanuts; find out if anyone in your group is allergic <u>before</u> you start this game.

WHAT YOU'LL NEED

- Two or more pounds of peanuts in their shells.
- Green, blue, and red markers (optional).
- Paper or plastic bags for every player.

HOW TO PLAY

The basic rules and strategy for hiding and hunting nuts are the same as for a fossil hunt (see pages 13–15). Whichever player or team finds the most nuts in thirty minutes wins.

For more excitement, draw green 2's on ten nuts, blue 5's on five, and a red X on one, leaving at least fifty nuts plain. The green nuts are worth two points, the blues are five, the red is ten, and all others are worth one. Whoever scores the most points wins.

Make sure that all the peanuts are still in their shells and that none of the shells has any cracks or holes to let in dirt or germs. Don't hide nuts anywhere that dogs or geese have turned into an outdoor toilet.

Jigsaw Hunt

Which treasure hunter will be first to find a complete puzzle and put it together, piece by piece?

WHO CAN PLAY
Two to six.

WHERE TO PLAY
Indoors is best, but outside is okay if the ground and grass are dry and it's not too windy.

WHAT YOU'LL NEED
- One picture for each hunter (see Setting Up).
- Scissors.
- Construction paper in different colors (optional).

SETTING UP
Get as many copies of the same picture as there are players. Choose a picture that doesn't have a lot of white space. You might use a set of identical postcards or greeting cards. If you have a computer with a color printer, you could scan a picture or find one in a program or on the Internet and then print identical copies onto thin card stock. Or draw a picture, write a message across it, and photocopy.

Stack the pictures neatly, and simultaneously cut them into nine pieces each with strong scissors to make a set of identical nine-piece puzzles, taking care that the pictures stay aligned as you cut them. Mix up the pieces; then hide each one separately so that at least a small part of every piece is visible, as in Fossil Hunt.

—2—
Worldwide Scavenger Hunt

Find triangles built on squares in a city
for the dead in a desert by a river.
(Answer found on p. 80)

HOW TO PLAY

Players hunt for pieces until somebody wins by assembling a complete puzzle. A player who finds two identical pieces can offer to trade one with anyone else. If nobody volunteers, the player can demand a trade and pick a piece, facedown, from the player who has collected the most pieces.

This game can also be prepared so that every player tries to complete a different puzzle. Paste or print each picture onto a different-colored sheet of construction paper before cutting into nine-piece puzzles as before, then mix up and hide the pieces. When each treasure hunter finds the first puzzle piece, she must call out the name of the color. From then on, she is looking only for pieces of that color. If she finds a piece that's another color, or if someone else finds a piece from a color that's already been claimed, the player leaves that piece where it is. Again, the winner is the first player to complete a puzzle.

Ice Hunt

Who says you can't have an outdoor treasure hunt on a snowy day? Use water and food coloring to make at least a dozen colored ice cubes.

Hide them in the snow; then let everybody go out with plastic bags to find them before the ice melts or the players freeze. And remember, don't eat yellow snow!

TREASURE HUNTS WITH CLUES

Puzzling out cryptic clues or mysterious maps that lead to treasure is exciting fun for anyone who's ever dreamed of adventure.

Follow the Clues

One hidden clue leads to the next, which leads to the next, and on and on till a treasure is found.

WHO CAN PLAY
Two to four are ideal, though more can join in.

WHERE TO PLAY
Indoors or out. The more rooms or outdoor areas you use, the harder and longer the hunt will be.

WHAT YOU'LL NEED
- A pen or pencil.
- Little slips of paper. (A pad of three-by-two-inch stick-on notes, such as Post-it notes, is best.)
- A treasure. This should be a small, distinctive, easily concealed object, such as a shiny stone or seashell, a piece of jewelry, or a bag of chocolate coins. Or just write "Treasure" or draw a treasure chest on a piece of paper.

SETTING UP
Find a good place to hide the treasure; then write a clue that leads straight to it. Hide the clue, then write and hide another clue that leads to that one, and so on. Try to hide each clue so that a small part of the paper shows, and don't hide clues too close together.

Use as many clues as you want, numbering them in order. Five or six good clues will make a hunt of about half an hour. Leave one clue unhidden to start the hunt.

WRITING CLUES

The best clues aren't too hard and aren't too easy. "Look in a book" won't narrow things down enough in a house filled with hundreds of books, and "Look on page 27 of The Secret Garden" is too easy, especially if The Secret Garden happens to be out on the coffee table. But "Look in a book in a great green room" may take a bit of thinking before treasure hunters set off in search of a copy of Goodnight Moon.

Use your sense of humor. Stick a clue to the bottom of a rocking chair, then lead to it with something like "Get down and rock."

It's even more fun if you can rhyme your clues. Hiding treasure inside the video of 101 Dalmatians? You could write:

Find a box with lots and lots
of pets with lots and lots of spots.

Sometimes working the clue number in makes it easier to find a rhyme:

Look at yourself and open a door
and there you'll find clue number four

suggests that the fourth clue is hidden behind a mirrored door.

HOW TO PLAY

All the treasure hunters should work together as one team. Let them know which areas or rooms are in and which are out-of-bounds; then read the first clue. They'll have to solve and follow clue after clue until they find the treasure. If the hunters get stuck for more than five minutes, it's okay to give extra hints like "warm" and "cold" to get the game moving again. Whoever finds the treasure can set up the next hunt.

TIPS FOR HUNTERS

Listen to clues carefully, and read them over a few times. Pay attention to every word, and try to think of different meanings. "Light" could mean a lamp or a flashlight or a matchbox, but it could also mean something that isn't dark or isn't heavy. It could also refer to a picture of a lighthouse hanging on the wall. "Keys" could be door keys or piano keys. Brainstorm with your fellow treasure hunters, and don't think you have to solve every clue all by yourself.

SAFETY

Don't hide or hunt for treasures or clues anyplace that might be dangerous, such as a light socket or lawn mower blade, or germ-ridden, such as the inside of a toilet bowl.

Treasure Fact

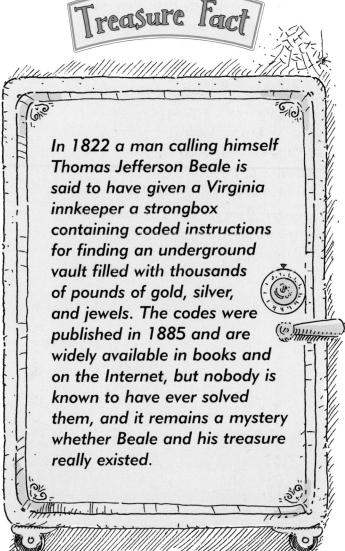

In 1822 a man calling himself Thomas Jefferson Beale is said to have given a Virginia innkeeper a strongbox containing coded instructions for finding an underground vault filled with thousands of pounds of gold, silver, and jewels. The codes were published in 1885 and are widely available in books and on the Internet, but nobody is known to have ever solved them, and it remains a mystery whether Beale and his treasure really existed.

Lots of Clues, Lots of Treasures

Following from clue to clue together isn't easy for a large group. But who says you can't have lots of clues leading to lots of different treasures?

WHO CAN PLAY

The more the merrier. You can divide the players into two or more teams if you like.

WHERE TO PLAY

Indoors or out. As always, let the players know which rooms or areas are in and out-of-bounds.

WHAT YOU'LL NEED

- Pencils and lists of clues (see Setting Up) for everyone.
- A dozen or more easily concealed treasures, such as chocolate coins, jewelry, shells, or pictures of treasure chests. If you're planning to give away the treasures as party favors, be sure to have extra favors for guests who don't find any on their own.

SETTING UP

Hide all the treasures separately. For each treasure, write one clue that leads straight to it (see pages 26 and 27 for tips on writing and solving clues). Write or type all the clues on a list, and make enough copies to go around for all the teams or players.

HOW TO PLAY

Give each player or team the list of clues; then let the players split up and try to be the first to find as many treasures as they can, in any order. Set a time limit of thirty minutes to an hour, depending on how many players and treasures there are. If all the hunters get stuck after a while, it's okay to call everyone together and give extra hints. If you've got a very competitive group, you can have a grand prize for the player or team that finds the most treasures.

TIPS FOR HUNTERS

Pay attention to what other players are doing so that you don't waste time looking for treasures that have already been found. Whenever a clue gets solved, check it off your list. Remember, you can look for the treasures in any order. Try to get the easiest ones out of the way first.

-3-
Worldwide Scavenger Hunt
In a U.S. city that isn't part of any state, the tallest building has just eight windows. This was once the tallest building in the world, and it is named after the same man as the city. What is the building?

(Answer found on p. 80)

29

House Hunt

How well do you know your own neighborhood? No need to hide treasures for this intriguing outdoor hunt.

WHO CAN PLAY

Two or more. Even observant four- and five-year-olds can join in as long as somebody supervises closely to make sure they don't run into the street.

WHERE TO PLAY

Any neighborhood, whether in a city, town, or suburb, where there are lots of different-looking houses or buildings on a single block.

WHAT YOU'LL NEED

- A pen or pencil and paper.

SETTING UP

Walk up and down the block, looking at each house, store, or building for features that stand out from everyplace else. Write up a list of clues for at least ten different addresses. For example:

- A toy giraffe in a window
- A chimney with four diamond-shaped holes along the top
- A red door with a green window
- A knocker shaped like a warthog

Don't make clues for things that might not still be there a few minutes later, such as a yellow-bellied sapsucker perched on a mailbox or a tattooed woman picking her nose on a front porch. Also, don't pick anything that isn't clearly visible from the sidewalk, such as a house with purple polka-dotted underpants hanging out to dry on the back porch or an apartment with a copy of the December issue of <u>Mad</u> magazine on the bed.

You can choose places on both sides of the street, especially if you're in a quiet neighborhood and the street isn't too wide. For an extra challenge, go all around the block, not just on the side that you live on. Either way, mix up the clues so that people have to keep going up and down or all around the block to find the right locations.

HOW TO PLAY

If just a few people are playing, hold on to the list, and read one clue at a time to the treasure hunters. If there's a big group, divide them into teams, and give each team or every player a copy of the whole list and a pen or pencil for writing down the street number that goes with each clue. Or divide into two teams, and give each team half an hour to make a list of ten clues for the other team and then another half hour for each team to spread out and solve as many of the other side's clues as possible. Whoever finds the most correct addresses wins the game.

-4-
Worldwide Scavenger Hunt

If I went on a tour and I fell three hundred meters and landed on the Field of Mars, where would I be?

(Answer found on p. 80)

SAFETY

Stay on the sidewalk—stepping out into the street to get a better view just isn't worth the risk.

31

Treasure Map

X marks the spot when you create a map that leads to treasure.

WHO CAN PLAY

Two or more—at least one to hide the treasure and make the map, plus one or more to hunt for the treasure.

WHERE TO PLAY

Outdoors, in a neighborhood, park, yard, or other area with lots of open space.

WHAT YOU'LL NEED

- A pen or pencil and paper for making the map.
- A treasure, preferably in a wooden or metal box.
- A tape measure and compass (optional).
- A shovel or trowel for burying the treasure (optional).

SETTING UP

First choose a place to hide the treasure, but don't hide it right away. A day or more before you're planning to hold the treasure hunt, make a rough but detailed map of the area within twenty or thirty feet of the hiding place, and let X mark the spot on the map. You might want to copy the map over when you get home to make it neater or even decorate it like an old pirate map. It's okay if you're not a great artist.

You can use a tape measure and compass to help pinpoint the treasure, but don't identify exactly where to start looking, or the hunt will be too easy. Draw a mailbox in the middle of a detailed pattern of six bushes, for example, but <u>don't</u> say that the mailbox and bushes are at the southeast corner of Thirty-fourth and Vine.

The morning of the treasure hunt, hide the treasure, making sure that nobody sees what you're doing. You can bury it (see below), stash it in a hedge or hollow, or hide it someplace where it can't be seen and where no one will stumble across it by accident.

BURIED TREASURE

For more excitement, why not bury the treasure? Choose a spot where you can dig about six inches to a foot down without disturbing the grass or other plants and where no one will notice. Place the treasure in the hole, cover it up, and mark the spot clearly but inconspicuously with a stick or stone with an X scratched on. You can also bury it beneath a board, flagstone, or other inconspicuous, easily removable marker.

HOW TO PLAY

Give the map to the treasure hunters, and let them search for landmarks they recognize from the map. The players can all work together, or you can make a copy of the map for each one and let the players or teams race to be the first to find the secret hiding place. If you've buried the treasure, make sure to give people a shovel or trowel to dig it up with.

Real-life pirate captains hardly ever buried the treasures they plundered. If they didn't share the loot to pay their crew, there was sure to be a mutiny.

Follow the Maps

For a longer, more challenging hunt, make a series of maps that lead from one hiding place to the next until the last map finally leads to the treasure. As with "Follow the Clues," the easiest way to do this is to start where you plan to hide the treasure and work backward from there. You can add written clues to the maps as well. For example, if you're burying treasure in your own backyard, the last map—the one that shows your yard—might feature a rebus or a math problem that leads to your address.

34

Follow the Compass

How good are you at giving and following directions? A trail of maps and clues leads to the treasure.

WHO CAN PLAY

Two or more.

WHERE TO PLAY

Outdoors is best, though you can adapt the game to play inside.

WHAT YOU'LL NEED

- A pen or pencil.
- A pad of paper or loose sheets and a clipboard.
- A treasure, preferably in a wooden or metal box.
- A tape measure.
- A compass.
- A shovel or trowel for burying the treasure (optional).

SETTING UP

First choose a place to hide the treasure, as in "Treasure Map." Find and go to a second hiding place within fifty feet of the treasure site; measure the distance and use the compass to determine the exact direction from the new hiding place to the treasure. Sketch a picture of the spot where the treasure is hidden, add the distance and direction, then fold up and hide this clue. Now find and go to a third hiding place within fifty feet of the second. Sketch the spot where the last clue is hidden, again add the distance and direction, then fold up and hide the clue. Working backward in this way, leave a trail of about five to ten clues, always making sure to show the compass direction <u>to</u> the next clue, not away from it.

HOW TO PLAY

Give the treasure hunters the compass, tape measure, and first clue, and let them track their way from clue to clue until they find the treasure.

Treasure Fact

In 1795 three young men found what looked like a ship's block and tackle dangling over a circle of settled ground in a clearing on tiny Oak Island off Nova Scotia. The boys had heard many tales of pirates hiding in the area, and, dreaming of buried treasure, they began digging what came to be known as the Money Pit. Since then six people have died, team after team has labored, and millions of dollars have been spent sinking hundred-foot holes all over the island, but nobody knows for certain what treasure, if any, was ever buried there.

SCAVENGER HUNTS

Indoors or out each team has a limited time to hunt up the most objects on a list. The game gets really wacky when teams make up each other's lists!

Indoor Scavenger Hunt

Just how much junk can you scout up around the house?

WHO CAN PLAY

Any number and any age. For four or more players, it's usually best to divide into teams.

WHERE TO PLAY

A house or an apartment, using as many rooms as possible. If you're in a house with a yard, you can open up the hunt to be both in- and out-of-doors. See "Nature Hunt" (page 42) for some examples of outdoor items to add to the list. And if neighborhood friends are playing with you, why not ask for permission to hunt in their houses or apartments as well as your own?

WHAT YOU'LL NEED

- Pencils.
- Lists of things (see Setting Up).
- Paper or plastic shopping bags.

SETTING UP

Make a list of at least twenty small items that might possibly be found around the home—the more hunters, the more items. Make the list specific enough to be challenging and fun without being impossible. Here are some suggestions to help you get started:

- A fortune cookie
- A cornflake at least an inch across
- A piece of moldy bread
- A pistachio nut in an uncracked shell
- A purple toothbrush
- A green feather
- The tube from a used-up roll of toilet paper
- A rubber duck that's any color but yellow
- A matchbook with a phone number on it
- A green pencil
- A birthday candle
- A spool of yellow thread

- A baby shoe no more than three inches long
- A sock with at least four different colors
- A quarter from the current year
- A dime from the 1960s
- A stamped postcard from another continent
- A paperback book by a woman with a Z in her name
- A baseball card of a player with an X in his name
- An album with all five vowels in the title

Make copies of the list for all the players or teams.

SAFETY

Keep dangerous items, such as bleach, insecticides, and carving knives, off the list. The same goes for glassware and other fragile things.

HOW TO PLAY

Give each player or team the list, a pencil, and a shopping bag, then let the players split up and try to collect as many items as they can, in any order. Set a time limit of thirty minutes to an hour, depending on how many players and items there are. When time's up, or if one team rounds up everything on the list ahead of time, the players gather to compare and count off how many items they found. Your family will appreciate it if you ask everyone to help put all items back where they belong after the hunt is over!

TIPS FOR HUNTERS

Read through the whole list carefully before you start hunting, and don't spend too much time focusing on any one item. Ask yourself which items are most likely to be found in each room.

COMPETITIVE LISTS

For a fun scavenger hunt with no advance preparation, divide all the players into two teams. Each team has ten or fifteen minutes to make up a list of thirty items for the other team to find. Give each team one hour to find as much as it can from the list its rivals made. After the players have gathered and counted how many items each team found, switch lists. Each team has just five minutes to take the list they created at the beginning and collect whatever the other team missed.

Treasure Fact

Every year teams of students at the University of Chicago compete in a four-day scavenger hunt featuring a list of more than three hundred items and stunts. Challenges have included finding a live elephant, making and eating the grossest pizza, and building a working nuclear breeder reactor.

Nature Hunt

Get in touch with nature by going on a scavenger hunt.

WHO CAN PLAY

Any number and any age. For four or more players, it's usually best to divide into teams.

WHERE TO PLAY

Outdoors in any yard, park, school yard, or other area where lots of things grow.

WHAT YOU'LL NEED

- Pencils.
- Lists of things (see Setting Up).
- Paper or plastic shopping bags.

SETTING UP

Make a list of at least twenty small, naturally occurring things that might be found in your area. Vary the list according to the season and to where the hunt is happening—shells and driftwood for the beach, for example. Put in enough specific details to make the hunt challenging without making it impossible, and make copies of the list for all the players or teams. Some possibilities are:

- A pink flower petal
- A yellow petal
- A petal with more than one color
- A complete acorn, including cap
- A dandelion flower

- A seedpod that rattles when it's shaken
- A spiny seed burr
- A maple leaf
- A red leaf
- A leaf with at least three colors
- A leaf an insect has chewed on
- A twig with white bark
- A twig with pine needles on it
- A long pinecone
- A round pinecone
- A gray feather
- A colorful feather
- A white pebble
- A blue pebble
- A stone shaped like an arrowhead

HOW TO PLAY

Give each player or team a list, bag, and pencil, then let the players split up and try to collect as many items as they can, in any order. Set a time limit of thirty minutes to an hour, depending on how many players and items there are.

TIPS FOR HUNTERS

Read through the whole list carefully before you start hunting, and don't spend too much time focusing on any one item. Also, please show respect for nature and for people's property— don't go trampling through gardens or yanking off flowers, leaves, and branches.

LEAF HUNT

No need to make lists to have a leaf hunt. Everybody sets out with collecting bags to see who can bring back the most different types of leaves in half an hour.

Treasure Fact

An abandoned garbage dump can be a real treasure trove. Bottles, buttons, old toys, and other trash left behind many years ago may now be rare and valuable collectors' items.

Magazine Hunt

You don't need much space for this rainy-day scavenger hunt—just stacks of old magazines.

WHO CAN PLAY

Any number, but two to four are best. Even preschoolers will enjoy playing.

WHERE TO PLAY

Indoors, with the players sitting around a table or in a circle on the floor.

WHAT YOU'LL NEED

- At least a dozen old magazines and catalogs rescued from the recycling pile, preferably ones with lots of photos. (Don't peek ahead inside the magazines if you're going to be playing yourself.)
- Scissors for everyone.
- Lists (see Setting Up).

SETTING UP

Make a list of at least twenty things or people to look for in the magazines, such as:

- A picture of the president
- A picture of the queen of England
- A scuba diver
- A clown
- A caveman
- A woman with a microphone in her hand
- An athlete wearing an odd-numbered uniform
- A child eating ice cream
- A baby wearing glasses
- A parrot
- A pterodactyl
- A dog and a cat in the same picture
- A turtle
- A lobster
- An ant
- A submarine
- A school bus
- A bicycle with training wheels
- A car that's painted at least three colors
- A tornado
- A volcano

You don't have to make up the list in advance. Why not get paper and pen or pencil, and let all the players take turns adding things to the list together before anyone peeks in the magazines.

46

HOW TO PLAY

Everyone has thirty minutes to an hour to find and clip as many different items from the list as he can. The pictures can be photos, drawings, or even toys, as long as they fit the descriptions. Different people can clip different pictures of the same item. Hunters can hold on to only one magazine at a time; after someone finishes with a magazine, it goes back in the middle for anyone else to claim. You might want to make it a rule that anytime someone clips a picture from a magazine, any other player with fewer clippings can demand to trade magazines.

TIPS FOR HUNTERS

Read through the whole list carefully; then flip through each magazine quickly to see if any pictures jump out at you. Start with whichever magazines look likeliest to have several of the items inside—nature magazines, for instance, if there are a lot of animals on the list.

Many serious treasure hunts start at the library, with researchers digging through old newspapers to learn about shipwrecks, battles, unsolved robberies, and other clues to long-forgotten treasures.

47

Number Hunt

Teams race around town to collect the numbers needed to answer a list of questions.

WHO CAN PLAY

Two or more teams of two to five players. This is a great game for matching family against family, but in any case <u>it is strongly recommended that each team include at least one adult</u>.

WHERE TO PLAY

Lots of different stores, restaurants, buildings, gas stations, and other public places. The hunt can be done on foot or bike if the locations are all in the same neighborhood; locations can be spread around town if each team has a car and driver or if you're in a city with good public transportation. This hunt can also be organized at school or camp, using rooms and sites all over the campus.

WHAT YOU'LL NEED

- Pencils and lists of questions for everyone.
- Maps and phone books to help players locate the places they need to go to.

SETTING UP

Make a list of at least ten questions. The answer to each question should be a number that can be determined by going to a different location. For example:

- How many flavors of ice cream are served at Yogi's Café?
- How much is a pound of kumquats at Fairway Supermarket?
- How much is a gallon of regular gasoline at Shell on Anderson Avenue?
- How many toilets in the rest rooms at the Burger King on Palisade Avenue?
- How many crystal chandeliers at the Silver Pond restaurant?
- How many stories high is Horizon House?
- How many buttons on a doorman's uniform at 300 Winston Drive?
- What is the address of the first red house on Abbott Boulevard, north of Route 5?
- How many windows on the front facade of Borough Hall?
- What's the phone number for the pay phone at the 7-Eleven at Whiteman Plaza?
- How many coin-operated copy machines at the public library?
- How many washing machines at Dirty Duds Done Dirt Cheap?
- How many chairs in Ms. Fox's class?
- What is the year on the oldest basketball trophy in the trophy case?
- How many tables in the lunchroom?

Make sure that all locations will be accessible when the hunt is scheduled to go on; if the Bonnie and Clyde National Bank closes on Sundays, for instance, don't expect players to break into the bank on a Sunday afternoon to find out how many cashiers' windows there are. Also, don't ask for numbers that could change any minute, such as the amount of time left on a certain parking meter or the number of flies hovering over a certain garbage can.

HOW TO PLAY

Give each team a copy of the list and a pencil; then send the teams out to try and find as many answers as they can within a time limit of one to two hours. At an agreed-upon time, everyone meets up to count off how many correct numbers they've found.

Everybody should agree at the start on whether to allow players to phone for information instead of visiting every location. No team should be allowed to use a cell phone unless every team has one.

TIPS FOR HUNTERS

Sit down with a map and phone book, and quickly plan the fastest possible route to reach all or most of the locations.

SAFETY

Don't dream up any questions that might put players into dangerous situations, such as "How many steps lead down to the sewer under the manhole cover in front of police headquarters?"

—5—
Worldwide Scavenger Hunt

Feel free to find a ring with a crack in the city of brotherly love.
(Answer found on p. 80)

What's the Difference?

Match your memory and your eye for detail against your friends'.

WHO CAN PLAY

Any number, but two to four are best.

WHERE TO PLAY

Indoors, in a single room. The best rooms for this game are well furnished, but not too messy.

HOW TO PLAY

All the players look around the room carefully for a few minutes, trying to memorize exactly where everything is. Then all but one player leave the room and close the door. The remaining player has five minutes to make ten visible changes in the room: curtains pulled, cabinets opened, furniture slid over, undies left dangling from the chandelier, and so on. The game's more fun if you mix some really wacky changes in with some more subtle ones. The other players return and try to spot all the differences, either competitively or as a group. Then someone else takes a turn to move ten things out of place.

51

TREASURE CHASES

These fast-moving games send players racing off after treasure—and one another.

Monster in the Maze

Get the money out of the maze before the monster gets you.

WHO CAN PLAY

Any number, but two at a time are best.

WHERE TO PLAY

Outdoors.

WHAT YOU'LL NEED

- Ten or more pennies.
- Choice of chalk;
  Masking tape;
  String, scissors, and two dozen
  sticks or stakes; or
  Eight or more pieces of movable patio
  furniture.

SETTING UP

Make a simple maze on the ground. Draw the "walls" with chalk, mark them with tape, or stake them with sticks and string. You can also make an obstacle course using lawn chairs and other patio furniture. The maze can be square or round as long as:

- It is about ten to fifteen feet across.
- The paths are wide enough to walk or run through without stepping over the lines.
- There's a clearly marked border around it with two exits on opposite sides.
- Every spot must be reachable from both exits even if there are dead-end paths.

HOW TO PLAY

Players take turns randomly scattering the coins throughout the maze. Everybody then takes turns being monsters and treasure hunters. First, a treasure hunter enters the maze and walks or runs through it, picking up any coins she can on her way to the other exit. The monster counts out loud to five, then follows and chases the treasure hunter through the maze. If the treasure hunter escapes, she gets to keep the coins she's picked up, but if the monster tags her, she must scatter all her coins in the maze again and take the next turn as monster. No player is allowed to step over any "wall" of the maze. Monsters can't reach over the walls to tag, but treasure hunters can reach over to grab coins. When all coins are out of the maze, the player with the most is the winner.

TIPS FOR HUNTERS

Glance ahead at the maze before you go in, and try to figure out the best path through it.

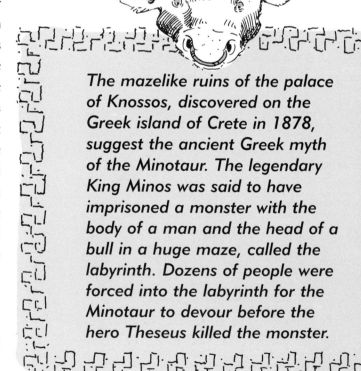

Treasure Fact

The mazelike ruins of the palace of Knossos, discovered on the Greek island of Crete in 1878, suggest the ancient Greek myth of the Minotaur. The legendary King Minos was said to have imprisoned a monster with the body of a man and the head of a bull in a huge maze, called the labyrinth. Dozens of people were forced into the labyrinth for the Minotaur to devour before the hero Theseus killed the monster.

Who's Got the Loot?

Try to guess who has the stolen loot—and catch him before he gets away.

WHO CAN PLAY

The more the merrier in two teams of at least four each.

WHERE TO PLAY

A playing field, a gym floor, or any other area at least twenty-five feet wide by fifty feet long.

WHAT YOU'LL NEED

- A medal or other treasurelike item that one of the players can hide in his pockets or around his neck.

HOW TO PLAY

Teams take turns being cops and robbers. The cops wait at one end of the field while the robbers take the medal or other treasure, go into a tight circle at the other end, and secretly pick one member of the team to carry the loot. She slips it in her pocket or hides it under her clothing so that the cops can't tell who has it. When the robbers are ready, they break their circle and start heading across the field. Now the cops can start chasing the robbers. Cops tag as many robbers as they can, and any robber who gets tagged is out of that round, but the only robber who really counts is the one hiding the loot. If she's tagged, the game stops and she has to hand over the loot, but if she makes it all the way across the field without being tagged, she waves the loot, and her team scores a point. Either way, the teams switch turns being robbers after every round. The first team to escape with the loot five times wins the game.

–6–
Worldwide Scavenger Hunt

High up on a mountain meet
four heads with no hands or feet.
All you need is thirty-one cents
to see the faces of three of these gents.

(Answer found on p. 80)

Follow the Arrows

Robbers leave cops a trail of treasures in this freewheeling outdoor chase.

WHO CAN PLAY

Any number divided into two teams.

WHERE TO PLAY

Outdoors in any neighborhood or park with lots of places to run around and hide safely.

WHAT YOU'LL NEED

- Colored chalk.
- Ten or more "treasures." These could be painted eggs, walnuts, oranges, or even cards that say "Treasure."
- Bags for each team to hold the treasures.

HOW TO PLAY

Teams take turns being cops and robbers. The robbers get a two-minute head start to steal away with the treasures and a piece of chalk while the cops look away or wait inside. The robbers must blaze a winding trail with arrows chalked about every ten yards or so to point which way they are heading. Along the way they drop or hide their treasures one at a time within two yards of some of the arrows. The cops follow the arrows and try to find and tag the robbers while picking up treasures along the way. If the cops catch the robbers, they score one point for each robber caught, one point for each treasure found on the way, and two points for each treasure the robbers haven't yet hidden. But if the robbers can wind their way back home without being caught by the cops, then the robbers score one point for each one of them who got home safely, one point for each treasure they're still carrying, and two points for any hidden treasures that the cops didn't find. Each team plays once as cops and once as robbers, using a different-colored chalk to avoid confusion. The team that scores the most points wins.

PAPER ARROWS

Instead of colored chalk, you can also have the robbers tape paper arrows along the trail for the cops to pick up. Cut out at least one hundred five-inch arrows before the game begins.

CAR AND BUS TREASURE HUNTS

Being in the backseat doesn't have to be boring—not when you can have a treasure hunt or scavenger hunt while you ride along.

Scavenger Road Trip

How much can you find just by looking out the window?

WHO CAN PLAY
Anybody with a view out the window of a moving vehicle.

WHAT YOU'LL NEED
* A list (see Setting Up) and a pen or pencil for every player.

SETTING UP

Make a list of at least twenty things that you might see out the window on your trip, such as:

- A rainbow
- A cow that isn't black and white
- A statue of someone riding a horse
- A horse riding in a truck or trailer
- A picture of a flying horse
- A helicopter
- Skywriting
- An ice-cream truck
- A train with at least three red cars
- A sailboat
- A water tower

- A man pushing a baby carriage
- A woman carrying a baby in a backpack
- A dog leaning its head out a car window
- An orange cat
- A bird on a power line
- A picture of a computer
- The number 13
- A billboard showing a cup of coffee
- A doughnut shop

Vary the list according to where you're going and the time of year; there's no point looking for snowmen in Hawaii or surfers in the Rocky Mountains. If you're on an airplane, you should probably include people and things that you might find or see inside the plane.

HOW TO PLAY

Players look out the windows for items on the list in any order. The first person to see something and call out what it is "collects" that item. Mark that player's name or initials by the item on the list; other players must wait till they see another example in a different place before they can call and collect it. (For a more challenging and competitive game, agree that only the first person who calls an item can collect it even if someone else spots another example of that item later.) Whoever collects the most items by the end of the ride is the winner.

Treasure Fact

The Oregon Trail and other routes that the pioneers took westward are littered with antiques, historical artifacts, rare coins, and other lost treasures. Families often loaded all their possessions into their covered wagons, only to have to abandon or hide their valuables along the way in order to lighten their load enough to make it safely across the mountains.

Motor Safari

Who can spot the most kinds of critters?

WHO CAN PLAY

Anybody with a view out the window of a moving car, bus, or train.

WHAT YOU'LL NEED

- Pens or pencils and paper.

SETTING UP

Draw up a sheet with different columns under each player's name, or give each player a pen or pencil and paper of his own.

HOW TO PLAY

Hunters must be on the lookout for any kind of animal other than humans. The first person to spot an animal and call out what it is scores that creature. Write the animal down in that player's column; nobody else can claim that kind of animal for the rest of the game. Whoever spots the most different kinds of animals by the end of the trip is the winner.

If you prefer a less fiercely competitive game, let two or more players claim the same kind of animal if they see it in two different places. Also, players should agree at the start whether to count pictures of animals from signs and billboards or only live animals.

DO NOT FEED WILDLIFE

-7-
Worldwide Scavenger Hunt

Look down from space and see a
wall that people can walk on and
horses can ride on.

(Answer found on p. 80)

Alphabet Hunt

Who can be first to hunt up the whole alphabet from A to Z?

WHO CAN PLAY

Anybody who knows the alphabet and has a view out the window of a moving car, bus, or train.

HOW TO PLAY

The object of the game is to spot all the letters, in order, on license plates, signs, billboards, or anywhere else outside the vehicle. (No opening

up a book or map to find that elusive X.) Players must call out each letter as they see it, and they can claim only one letter at a time; if you pass a billboard for ABC Defrosters at the start of the game, for example, you can only call out A. Each player must work separately through the entire alphabet until somebody wins by reaching Z.

For fun without winners and losers, everybody can hunt the alphabet together. After one player finds A, somebody else has to find B, and so on, taking turns, until Z is reached.

TIPS FOR HUNTERS

You won't find Q on many license plates. Try looking for "quick" or "queen" on signs or store names. For X, your best bet might be "exit," "Exxon," or "taxi."

Treasure hunters with metal detectors often search along old roads and railroad tracks for rare coins and artifacts that travelers may have dropped many years before.

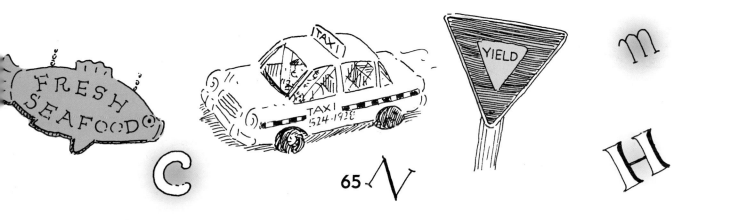

License Plate Hunt

Who can find the most plates from the most states?

WHO CAN PLAY

Anybody who can read and has a view out the window of a moving car or bus.

WHAT YOU'LL NEED

- Pens or pencils and paper.

SETTING UP

Draw up a sheet with different columns under each player's name, or give each player a pen or pencil and paper of her own.

HOW TO PLAY

Players race to be the first to call out the name of every state or province they see on license plates. Write that state down in the player's column. (You may want to play that once a state's been called, nobody else can claim it.) The first player to collect ten or fifteen different states or provinces is the winner, or if you prefer, it can be the player who collects the most different places by the end of the trip.

—8—
Worldwide Scavenger Hunt
Find a horseshoe in a horseshoe in a circle in a circle, and you'll see a famous English rock group.
(Answer found on p. 80)

Find It on the Map

"Do you know the way to San Jose?"

WHO CAN PLAY

Two are best, though more can play.

WHERE TO PLAY

Anywhere, with or without a view, as long as there's enough light to read.

WHAT YOU'LL NEED

- Road maps.
- Paper and pencils.

HOW TO PLAY

Each player takes a map and makes a list of ten places from it: towns, rivers, mountains, whatever. The players exchange maps and lists. Whoever is the first to locate all the places on the other player's list is the winner. The game's more fun and challenging if players can't peek at the map index.

Treasure Fact

Modern treasure hunters compare old maps with recent ones to locate ghost towns, deserted fairgrounds, and other places where people may have lost or abandoned things long ago.

68

OTHER TREASURE HUNTING GAMES

Have you ever gone hunting with a camera or a computer? Check out these thoroughly modern treasure hunts.

Photo Safari

Shoot as many animals as you can find—with a camera, of course. This hunt is more expensive to mount than most of the others in the book, and it takes patience to wait for the pictures to be developed, but photo safaris make very memorable outings, parties, or school activities.

WHO CAN PLAY
Any number. Budget about six to ten dollars per person for film and processing.

WHERE TO PLAY
Outdoors in any neighborhood, park, or other area that's full of living things and where hunters can walk around safely. Spring and fall are usually when you'll see the most animals; be sure everyone brings water and sunblock if you go out during the hottest days of summer.

Photo safaris are a great group activity for schools and summer camps. When the pictures come back from the developer, everyone can make posters, murals, or scrapbooks documenting all the local flora and fauna they captured on camera.

WHAT YOU'LL NEED

- A camera for each player. Unless you're playing with a bunch of shutterbugs who are bringing their own equipment, you'll need to buy single-use cameras for every person or team. Disposable cameras usually come loaded with film for twenty-seven pictures and sell for between five and ten dollars, but supermarkets often feature them for as low as three dollars each, so plan ahead and shop around. More expensive disposables may come with flash attachments, which can be useful for taking pictures in dark, shadowy places but aren't generally necessary for this game.

SETTING UP

Write each hunter's name on his camera, and use the first shot to take that person's picture, so that the films won't be mixed up later.

SAFETY

Players should hunt in groups of two to four if the hunt is going to take place over a large area. Find out if it's in an area with ticks, and warn everyone to take precautions against Lyme disease.

HOW TO PLAY

Hand out the cameras, and explain how to use them. Everybody will have one hour in which to take pictures of as many different kinds of animals and wildflowers as possible. The animals must be alive; photos of signs or of people don't count. Players can agree that it's all right to take pictures of different breeds of dogs or even different colors of horses for this safari, but everybody should try not to take more than one picture of the same animal or pictures of two identical animals.

When the hour is up, the hunters meet up to compare notes. If any players still haven't used all the film in their cameras, they can finish their rolls by shooting pictures of one another. Collect the cameras, and take them to a developer. (One-hour processing, at about ten dollars per roll, can add up to a lot of money, but overnight or second-day processing can usually be done for under five dollars for a single set of prints.) Get everyone together again, if possible, to hand out the pictures. This doesn't have to be a competitive game, but if you are giving out prizes, the winner is the hunter with pictures of the most kinds of animals and flowers.

Follow these pointers if you're new to photography.

USING THE CAMERA

Advance the film before shooting each picture by turning the dial on the back of most single-use cameras with your right thumb until it won't go any farther. Look carefully through the viewfinder in the back to select your shot. Hold the camera steady with both hands, and push the shutter release button on top with your right index finger to snap the picture. A counter on top usually shows the number of pictures remaining to be taken.

TAKING BETTER PICTURES

Always make sure that the sun is behind you or beside you when you take outdoor photos, or your picture may wind up showing nothing but a silhouette. Use the viewfinder to frame the subject of your picture carefully. If it doesn't all fit, you'll need to step back. If you can hardly see it, get closer—but never closer than four feet. If things are in the way, move to one side. If your subject blends in with its background, try a different angle. Remember that it's often a good idea to stand your camera on end for shots of people, trees, and other subjects that are more tall than wide.

PHOTOGRAPHING NATURE

Photographing nature takes patience. Practice by taking a few shots of flowers before you move on to animals. Approach animals quietly, and don't try to get too close. You may have only a second or two to get the shot, so wind your film in advance. If the animal is moving, your best chance for a good picture is to follow it through the viewfinder, then snap the shot as the creature changes direction.

DIFFICULT SHOTS

You won't be able to photograph every animal you find, so always make sure you can see your subject clearly through the viewfinder. Don't waste film on fish in the water; your photo won't show anything but mud. Ants and most other bugs are too small to show up unless you have a camera with a special lens. Sometimes you can take good pictures of butterflies, dragonflies, and other big bugs if you stand about four feet away and position yourself so that the bug contrasts with its background. A bee on a flower can make a nice shot, and as long as the bee is busy with the flower, it won't think of stinging you.

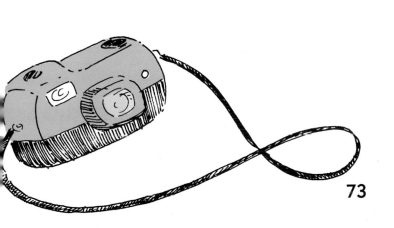

73

If you like to use a camcorder, try a video safari. Make your own half-hour nature documentary featuring all the animals you can capture on tape in your neighborhood.

SMILE, BUTTERCUP!

–9–
Worldwide Scavenger Hunt
Falling water spans a border where the Horseshoe meets the Goat. See it from a Rainbow Bridge or from a misty maiden boat.

(Answer found on p. 80)

Internet Scavenger Hunt

Surf the Web to hunt for trivia.

WHO CAN PLAY

Any number.

WHERE TO PLAY

Cyberspace.

WHAT YOU'LL NEED

- Internet connections for all players.

HOW TO PLAY

Each player makes a list of at least ten useless but fascinating bits of information that might be found by searching the Internet, such as:

- The number of lifeboats on the <u>Titanic</u>
- The zip code of the White House
- Where and when archaeopteryx was first discovered
- The seating capacity of the Hollywood Bowl
- The birthdays of all the Spice Girls
- The number of times Mark McGwire struck out in 1998
- The name of the South African minister of environmental affairs
- Where Beverly Cleary went to college
- The Newbery Medal winner for the year you were born
- The Academy Award winner for Best Song from twenty years ago

The players all give copies of their lists to one another, then all of them rush off to their computers to hunt for as many answers as they can find. Agree on a time limit. It can be an hour or an evening for a two-player game or a whole week if there are lots of players and a list of fifty or more items.

Players should agree in advance whether answers need to include web links or not. Sometimes it can take hours of combing through the Internet to locate facts that could be found in a minute using the index of any almanac. Web sites frequently contain misleading or false information, often copied directly from other sites, so don't be surprised if you and your friends come up with different answers to the same question.

Treasure Fact

Many scavenger hunts can be found on the Internet. Check out Lycos CyberSurfari at www.cybersurfari.org for an ongoing series of hunts leading to lots of fun sites.

TIPS FOR HUNTERS

A search for a word like "Titanic" may lead to almost a million web pages. Most search engines let you use plus and minus signs to narrow your search. Searching "+Titanic +lifeboats" still calls up almost twenty thousand pages. Eliminate sites about the motion picture with "−movie" and you're down to a mere twelve thousand. Suggest a list of technical features about the ship by adding "+specifications," and you've got a more manageable fifty or so. Click on a web page that looks promising from its capsule description; then use the "find" command (typically Control-F) to search within that page for the word "lifeboats."

Another approach is to search for "+Titanic +links." This will give you pages listing selected links, often with useful commentary, to sites about your subject.

Click Here

Find

–10–
Worldwide Scavenger Hunt

Save eight thousand miles with a fifty-mile shortcut that opened in 1914.
(Answer found on p. 80)

FURTHER READING

Books About Treasures and Treasure Hunting

Crooker, William S. Oak Island Gold. Halifax, NS: Nimbus, 1993.

Deem, James M. How to Hunt Buried Treasure. Boston: Houghton Mifflin, 1992.

Madison, Arnold. Lost Treasures of America. Chicago: Rand McNally, 1977.

Marx, Robert F. Buried Treasures You Can Find. Dallas: Ram, 1993.

National Geographic Society. Hidden Treasures of the Sea. Washington, DC:
    National Geographic Society, 1988.

Reid, Struan. The Children's Atlas of Lost Treasures. Brookfield, CT: Millbrook, 1997.

Thompson, Tommy. America's Lost Treasure. New York: Atlantic Monthly Press, 1998.

Titler, Dale M. Unnatural Resources: True Stories of American Treasure. Englewood Cliffs, NJ:
    Prentice-Hall, 1973.

Books About Games

Barry, Sheila Anne, and Doug Anderson. The World's Best Party Games. New York: Sterling,
    1987.

Brokaw, Meredith, and Annie Gilbar. The Penny Whistle Party Planner. New York:
    Simon and Schuster, 1991.

————. The Penny Whistle Traveling With Kids Book. New York: Simon and Schuster, 1995.

Burgett, Gordon. Treasure and Scavenger Hunts: How to Plan, Create, and Give Them.
    Santa Maria, CA: Communication Unlimited, 1994.

Cole, Joanna, and Stephanie Calmenson. Fun on the Run: Travel Games and Songs.
    New York: Morrow, 1999.

Hamilton, Leslie. Child's Play 6–12: 160 Instant Activities, Crafts, and Science Projects for
    Grade Schoolers. New York: Crown, 1991.

Salter, Richard, and Irene Prokop. Are We There Yet? Travel Games for Kids. New York:
    Prince, 1991.

INTERNET RESOURCES

Here are some web sites that you may find useful if you want to learn more about treasure hunting or about some of the facts in this book. Internet addresses change constantly, so please write to me in care of the publisher if you find any out-of-date information or if you discover new sites to recommend.

treasurehunt.about.com
The Treasure Hunting, Metal Detecting, Gold Prospecting home page for About.com is a good place to start mining the Internet for information about these topics, with hundreds of useful links as well as indexes to lost treasures in all fifty states.

www.nationalgeo.com
The National Geographic Society, publisher of <u>National Geographic</u> magazine, has many treasure-related games and activities, such as exploring sunken ships or ancient ruins, on its web site. Periodically the site features live, interactive coverage of expeditions to recover lost treasure.

www.losttreasure.com
The web site for <u>Lost Treasure</u> magazine features a menu of tales and treasure hunting tips that changes daily, as well as many on-line forums and a state-by-state directory of treasure hunting clubs and associations.

www.treasurenet.com
TreasureNet features links to sellers of metal detectors and other treasure hunting equipment, as well as the on-line home of <u>Western and Eastern Treasures</u> magazine.

www.discoveryquest.com
A collection of on-line forums for treasure hunters.

209.75.209.46
The Transnational Treasure Hunting Net contains many useful articles and forums.

WORLDWIDE SCAVENGER HUNT ANSWERS

—1

The Statue of Liberty, a gift from the people of France to the people of the United States, was completed in New York harbor in 1886.

—2

The pyramids at Giza, Egypt, were constructed near the Nile around 4,500 years ago to house the tombs of the pharaohs Khufu, Khafre, and Menkaure.

—3

The Washington Monument, completed in 1884, was the world's tallest structure at 555 feet until the completion of the Eiffel Tower.

—4

The Eiffel Tower (French, Tour Eiffel) was constructed in 1889 in Paris by Gustave Eiffel, the engineer who also helped to build the Statue of Liberty. Towering 984 feet (300 meters) over the park known as Champ de Mars (Field of Mars), this was the world's tallest building until 1930.

—5

The Liberty Bell, which used to hang in Philadelphia in the building now known as Independence Hall, was rung on July 8, 1776, to announce the first public reading of the Declaration of Independence. It cracked for the last time on Washington's birthday in 1846.

—6

Mount Rushmore in South Dakota features the sculpted heads of presidents George Washington, Thomas Jefferson, Abraham Lincoln, and Theodore Roosevelt.

—7

The Great Wall of China, which extends for as much as 1,500 miles, has been viewed from the Space Shuttle, though not, as many people believe, from the moon. The wall was built to be wide enough in many places for soldiers on horseback to gallop from one watchtower to the next.

—8

Stonehenge, the mysterious ancient monument that stands on England's Salisbury Plain, appears to have been constructed as a kind of a gigantic stone calendar.

—9

Niagara Falls is split by Goat Island, with the Canadian—or Horseshoe—Falls on one side and the American Falls on the other. Maid of the Mist tour boats sail up the Niagara River to the foot of the falls, and the Rainbow Bridge connects New York State and Ontario, Canada, just downstream.

—10

The Panama Canal joins the Atlantic and Pacific oceans, making it possible for about 13,000 ships a year to avoid having to sail all the away around South America.

80